Roots

PENGUIN
ENTERPRISE

An imprint of Penguin Random House

Penguine Enterprise
Penguin Enterprise is an imprint of the Penguin Random House group of companies whose addresses can be found at global.penguinrandomhouse.com
Published by Penguin Random House India Pvt. Ltd 4th Floor, Capital Tower 1, MG Road, Gurugram 122 002, Haryana, India

First published in Penguin Enterprise by Penguin Random House India 2024

10 9 8 7 6 5 4 3 2 1

ISBN 9780143473336

Typeset in Eldwin Script Light
Printed at Replika Press Pvt. Ltd, India

This book is dedicated to
Mom, Dad, Ammi, Dadu, Nani, and Nanu.
Thank you for showing me
my roots.

Roots

Avantika Swali

I think sometimes we only think forward. We look to the future, imagining we'll reach there soon. But I think we should look in all directions. Forward, straight, diagonal, to the side, and backward. This is a book about wanderers, curious ones, who backpack across India as discoverers, a country filled with more art and wonder than we could ever imagine. The four friends are creatures: a monkey, a tiger, a mouse, and an elephant. They find love in friendship.

First you'll meet Teesta, a monkey. She has a curious and inquisitive mind, always diving into problems and seeking answers to the world's mysteries, with a special love for math. Dance is her passion; it's how she expresses herself and works through her thoughts. Teesta, with her empathetic heart, is the centre of the group and a strong leader. Whether brainstorming or dancing, she's always there, asking questions.

You will also meet Kumbi, a big tiger. Despite his fierce appearance, Kumbi has a soft and fluffy inside. He's strong but terrified of butterflies, and gives the best big, warm hugs. Kumbi has a knack for finding the cosiest spots to nap, relishing moments of rest amid adventures. With his colourful mind, he can create or cook anything (a true foodie), turning ordinary things into something more. He loves to cook but loves to eat even more.

Then, you'll meet Vayu, a tiny mouse. Though she is small, her spirit is fearless, often the bravest member of the group. She invents the craziest plans to save the day, and her creativity captivates everyone near her. She's proud and excited, which can sometimes lead to trouble, but her loyalty is unwavering and she stands by her friends no matter what.

Finally, you will meet Raaho, a huge elephant who takes care of all of his friends. He carries the wisdom of ages, having lived a long life filled with stories. As a gentle giant, he is always ready with a listening ear and advice, sharing ancient tales of wisdom and custom to deepen his friends' understanding of the world. His love for storytelling shines during the nights, where he captivates his friends with tales from his past, often weaving in life lessons, though he does have a tendency to ramble.

Together, their journey spans the country, uncovering the rich cultural heritage of each place they visit. They begin in the Bandhavgarh forest of Madhya Pradesh, exploring the intricate patterns of Gond, then move to Bihar, where they are captivated by the vibrant colours of Madhubani. In Odisha, they marvel at the skill behind Ikat weaving before taking a boat through the Bay of Bengal to Mumbai to discover the beauty of Warli art.

The sparkling mirror work of Abla in Gujarat dazzles them next, followed by the bold block printing of Rajasthan. Punjab introduces them to the colourful embroidery of Phulkari, and in Lucknow, they are awed by the luxurious Zardozi craft. Finally, they return home, to their tree, in the Bandhavgarh forest of Madhya Pradesh.

These characters, these friends have made the journey feel real for me. I see myself, and those I love, reflect-ed in each one. I hope they inspire you to explore, or to look in some more directions as they take you along with them.

Lots of love,
Avantika

"hello"
"ouch"

"That's huge"

"How did the tree grow so tall and wide?"

"because its roots are so deep"
"hmm"

"Where are my roots?
I have only claws"

"We all have roots.
Roots are who we are
and where we come from"

"Wait! Where are you going?"

Kumbi turns around
and says, as if it were
obvious,
"To find my roots."

As an
afterthought,
he adds,
"Want to come with?"

"Good day."
"Hello."

"Do you know who I am
and where I come from?"

"I'm looking for my roots."

"This is who you are."

"Wait, my tail isn't blue."

"Sometimes art isn't exactly what's
real;
sometimes it's just to express
what you feel and
do what makes you happy.
My grandma taught me to paint like this.
The art is called Gond."

"My grandma taught me to hang from my tail."

"Our ancestors often show
us who we are."

"My grandmother taught me to paint
and be free but
to always know my roots."

"I am from the Gond Tribe and belong to nature and the forest. Just like you!"

"I am also an artist just like my grandma. We tell our stories and celebrate our culture with art - through our colourful patterns, animals and forests."

"Bye."

"I like my blue tail."

"I'm a bit tired."

"There's no hurry."

"Let's take a nap."

"Look, a house."
"Oh! it's hot!"

"It's so beautiful, we all need to look after it," said Teesta.

“Hello.”

“Good day.”

"Would you like to come in?
I have Khaja and tea."

"Wooow."
"This art is called Madhubani."

“The colours
are different.”

The artist walks to the kitchen,
“Yes. I made them myself.”

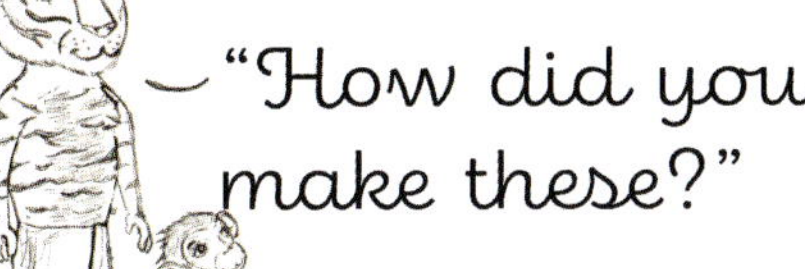

"Well all my colours are taken from nature. I make these colours from flowers, leaves and wild berries, but my favourite is this blue that I make from the Aparajita flower that grows just outside!"

"Noo, I meant the food."

"Wait! Tell us about you and your paintings. We are trying to learn about our roots!"

"Madhubani is like a magical storybook painted on walls or now, even on paper. I come from Madhubani, where we have all painted these pictures for hundreds of years. Our art is full of bright colours and scenes from nature with animals, birds and flowers. Long long ago the women of Madhubani started to decorate their homes with this art, but today, it is known in all the world for the life it brings and the stories it tells. Did you know that Madhu means honey and ban means forest? We want to share the sweetness of our forests with everyone! This is our culture."

"Thank you for sharing."

"Oh! It's starting to rain."

“What are they doing?”

"Thank you."

"What are you making?"

"I am weaving.
I am a weaver."

"Okay."
"Why is there a hole in your floor?"
"Is it for your roots?"

"It's a pit. For my pitloom."

"I use it to weave."

"And it is for my roots because my father used the same one."

“Wow.”

"This is Ikat, a weaving form with strong roots across our nation, but there are many different types in different places. Our cloth is very special because it's very very detailed and requires a lot of skill and time because we weave loose threads after dyeing them."

"I'd like to give you something."

"Thank you."

BAY OF BENGAL

"I'm scared."
"That's okay. We're here together."

"I'm Vayu."

"Good day."

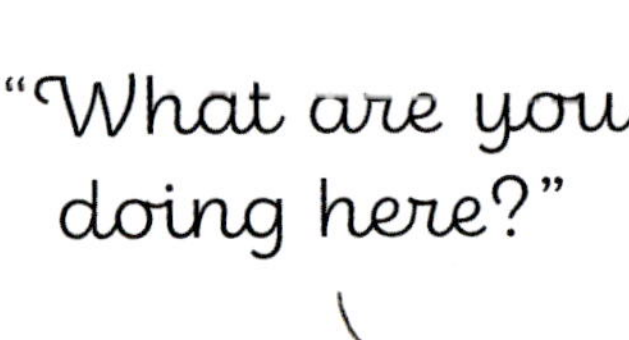

"We're looking for our roots."

"Did you lose them?"

"No, our roots are a part of us; we're just trying to discover what they are."

"How do I find out what my roots are?"

"Come with us."

"We've come a long way."

"I think I may be
missing home."

"Home can be anywhere;
come, I'll take you."

SANJAY GANDHI
NATIONAL PARK

"Wow!
It looks like home"
"Look!
He's like me!"

"Good day."
"Who are you?"

"Kumbi"
"Okay."
"Teesta"
"Vayu"

"What are you doing?"
"I'm painting like my grandma taught me. This is for her birthday."

"Can you teach us?"

The 3 continue to paint
and the girl begins to talk...

Warli is like a story told through shapes and patterns. We bring people and their stories to life on walls, and now, even on canvas. My grandma and I are from the Warli tribe; we have painted our lives for hundreds of years. I think simple things become special when you paint them. We use lots of earthy colours, and our people are made from circles, triangles and lines, all connected to the world around us. It's like a story of harmony, our community, and our love for nature.

"It takes a long time
to learn a craft."

"Thank you."

"Would you like to buy it?"
"What's this?"

"Yes! I would love to, but we don't have any money."

"We can give you this painting we made."
"Wow! Warli!"

"You know about Warli?"

"Yes, of course, Warli is an important art, and I'm an artisan."

"Look! There are so many mes!
And so many yous!"

The artisan explains the...

Mirror work is like capturing stars in fabric. We have been enhancing our textiles with mirrors for generations, to be full of colour and sparkle to reflect the best parts of all of us. Like you, when you can see yourself and all your friends. Each stitch keeps our traditions alive, reflecting their brightness and showing us the world's beauty.

“There is so much art everywhere.”

“Our roots have so much art.”

"Wow."

"thump,
thump,
thump"

"Ooooooops!"
"Oops!"

"hello."

"It's okay!"

“What are you doing?”

"We're exploring our roots,"

"We're block printers.
We have a big order of our
printed fabric coming up soon."

"Wow!"

"thump"

"I block printed you."

"That suits you,
Kumbi"

"Yes, block printing creates the most beautiful effect"

We hand-carve each wooden block, and each print tells a story of our craftsmanship. With these blocks we can make anything, in beautiful styles and colours, but our prints are often inspired by nature, with beautiful flowers, leaves, and animals. It is precise work, and we have to be careful, but it is also really fun to be able to work with your craft, your art and your friends every day.

"Wow"

"Bye."

"I'm a bit tired"

“Where to next!?!?”

"Do you need a ride?"

"I'm happy to help."

"Thank you!"

"I'm Raaho."

"Kumbi"
"Teesta"
"Vayu"

"Thank you"

"Where are you taking us?"

"Where my legs take me."

"Aahhhh ahhhh a butterfly!!"

"I hear music, maybe that will bring us all together."

"KUMBI!"

"We missed you."

"Look! The music!"

"We are doing what we love."
"We are practising our craft."
"We are making art."

"Wow."

Our craft is called Phulkari. It reminds me of a garden blooming on fabric. Our craft is all about bright, bold patterns stitched, turning everything bright, colourful and vibrant. 'Phulkari' means 'flower work, and the thread is like petals dancing on fabric.

"One thing means so much..."

Vayu ties a bow around each of their ears.

"Now we're matching."

"Bye."

"Wow! Everything's
so bright!"
"We're in a
special place."

"Let's follow the light!"
"I wonder what makes it shine"
"Well, we should always look for answers, it deepens our knowledge"

"Good day"
"Hello!"

"We love your shiny work"

The artist says "Oh! Thank you!
My grandmother taught me
how to make special craft
like this.

She was the first woman in
this city to learn. It was
hard but we must
follow our dreams."

"Wow." the four say
awestruck.

Zardozi is like weaving gold into fabric, turning cloth into something regal and special. I come from a place where this luxurious art of embroidery has been passed down for centuries. Our art uses fine gold and silver threads to create intricate patterns, we use it for the finest garments and accessories across the world. But most importantly, each of these stitices tells a story of heritage, which makes it fit for kings and queens.

"We loved hearing your story."
"I loved sharing it."

"Now you'll always
remember who you are."

"I think I know who I am now."

"I'm ready to go home."
"Where's home?"

"Where we feel safest,
loved and connected
to our roots."

“Then my home is right here, with you all.”

"Look, our roots."

"We have to make sure they stay strong so they can grow and grow."

"and grow."

Lucknow
Zardozi
Punjab
Phulkari
Rajasthan
Block print
Abla
Gujarat

Madhya Pradesh
Gond
Bihar
Madhubani
JOURNEY BEGINS
Odisha
Ikat
Mumbai
Warli
Bay of Bengal

In Gratitude

Endless gratitude to everyone who made this book a reality. To all of you who read it—thank you from the bottom of my heart. I poured so much love into these stories, these characters, and the craft that weaves through them. I hope the journey of the four friends has brought you even half as much joy as it brought me.

To my incredible family—thank you, again, for showing me my 'roots,' for opening my eyes to the wonders of our country's craft and culture. Thank you for inspiring this book.

I am profoundly grateful to the craft communities across India, whose timeless traditions and stories have been a constant source of inspiration and learning for me. Their skill and dedication is incredible, passed down through generations, to keep this intangible cultural legacy alive—this book exists because of their stories.

A million thank yous to Joohi Mehta, the amazing artist who brought these characters to life in ways I could only dream of. You've given Raaho wisdom in his eyes, Kumbi warmth in his hugs, Teesta brilliance in her voice, and Vayu endless energy in her tail. Thank you for bringing my thoughts to life.

To my mentor, Renuka Modi, thank you for your constant guidance. Renuka Aunty, you've shown me what it means to write with heart, and you've encouraged me every step of the way.

To my mentor, Sapna Kar—thank you, Sapna Aunty, for your forever support. You introduced me to the depth of craft and culture, and I'm forever grateful for everything you have done.

To my friends, thank you for being excited with me and for patiently enduring all my brainstorming sessions and countless trains of thought. You guys mean the world to me.

And to Penguin, thank you for believing in this book. I am truly honoured.

Finally, to my mom and dad—thank you for making every one of my dreams, each and every one, come true.

About the Author

Avantika Swali is a passionate artist and student who believes in her generation's potential to shape a more compassionate and creative future. In 2014, she founded ACE, a not-for-profit organisation dedicated to providing children with holistic education. Continuing this mission, she launched the ACE Book Club in 2021, a mobile library service aimed at democratising access to cultural and educational experiences for children. Later that year, Avantika co-founded Moonray, a contemporary fashion line focused on preserving traditional crafts through innovative design and collaboration. Roots is Avantika's debut book, created to inspire young readers and curious minds to explore the rich and diverse cultural heritage of India.